CAtomic Habits. Copyright © 2024 by Kitty Books

ISBN: 978-91-89848-90-0

All Rights Reserved. No part of this work may be reproduced, incorporated into a computer system, or transmitted in any form or by any means (electronic, mechanical, photocopying, recording or otherwise) without the prior written permission of the copyright holders. Infringement of such rights may constitute an intellectual property crime.

CAtomic Habits

by Kitty Books

The key to habit change is making the cue obvious—like how I meow at 4 a.m. when I want food.

Subtlety is overrated when it comes to making progress—or waking humans.

You don't rise to the level of your goals; you fall to the level of your routines. And your routine currently screams 'snooze button.'

Establish systems, not just dreams. I know this—I nap like it's a career.

Your brain fights change. Mine fights the vacuum cleaner.

Resistance to change is normal. Push through anyway—or hiss at it for fun.

Small wins lead to big changes. Unless you're me, in which case, I just knock the big stuff over.

Progress isn't linear, but chaos? That's always consistent.

The easiest habits to keep are the ones that make you look good. Like me, always camera-ready.

Vanity can be a motivator—don't underestimate it.

The brain loves habits—it's lazy like that. Just like me.

Your mind craves efficiency. Train it, or it'll just take naps instead.

Tracking progress helps. I track your every move from the top of the fridge.

Visibility drives accountability, whether it's for goals or stalking.

There's no such thing as 'too small to matter.' Just ask the hairball I left on your carpet.

Even the smallest actions have consequences, for better or worse.

If you think about it, habits are just routines that don't need approval. Like me at dinner time.

Simplify decision-making by turning good actions into reflexes.

Change is uncomfortable. Like trying to nap in a clean, fur-free bed.

Step out of your comfort zone—progress lives there, even if it's unfamiliar.

Habits thrive on rewards. My reward is making you think I care.

Reinforce good behavior—just don't expect sincerity.

Motivation gets you started; habits keep you going. Or, in my case, the smell of chicken.

Build systems so you don't rely on fleeting energy—or cravings.

The best time to start was yesterday. The second-best time is after my nap.

Procrastination kills progress. But sometimes naps are valid.

A messy start is still a start. Just look at me, knocking everything off the table before I get comfy.

Imperfect action beats perfect inaction every time. Start messy if you must.

Habits fail when you rely on willpower alone. Like me, failing to resist your sandwich.

Automation beats temptation. Structure your life to remove resistance.

It's not failure; it's feedback. Like when I miss a jump and pretend it was intentional.

Reframe mistakes as learning moments. Or just act cool about them.

Small cues lead to big actions. Like that one time you left the tuna can within reach.

Attention to detail pays off—whether for progress or mischief.

Your habits should align with your values. Unless your value is ignoring boundaries like me.

Know your why. Or just fake it with confidence.

Your future self is watching, so maybe stop procrastinating. Or do what I do: stare blankly out a window.

What you do today affects tomorrow. Unless you're napping.

Make bad habits harder. Unless that habit is opening doors, in which case I'll find a way.

Add friction to the things you want to stop. Just hope no one as clever as me is involved.

Big changes arise from small decisions, like choosing to sit on your favorite sweater.

Your habits reflect your choices, even the most furtive ones.

The right habit can be like catnip for the soul. Addictive and a little ridiculous, but hey, it works.

Find habits that energize you and make life better. Bonus if they're fun.

The best habits are invisible. Like the one where I shed fur on everything you own.

When habits blend into your life, they're harder to break—or notice.

It's not about the habit you want; it's about becoming someone who deserves it. Like me, deserving your food.

Focus on growth, not entitlement—though sometimes entitlement is yummy.

Good habits require effort upfront. Like me opening a cupboard just to nap inside.

The setup might be hard, but the payoff is worth it. Comfort is priceless.

Habits are contagious. Which is why I've trained you to mimic my every whim.

Surround yourself with people or things that embody what you aspire to—or just let them adapt to you.

You only need to improve by 1% each day. Like how I gradually ruin your furniture one paw at a time.

Small changes add up fast, for better or worse.

Start small and grow big. Or just go straight to knocking over the biggest vase.

Bold moves can work—but they're riskier than steady progress.

Every habit should serve a purpose. Mine is being adorable so you can't stay mad at me.

Align your actions with your goals. Bonus points if they make people forgive you.

Discipline isn't about restriction; it's about direction. Mine just happens to be towards chaos.

You can't control everything, but you can control your path. Unless you're chasing a laser pointer.

Habits stick when they're rewarding. Like the satisfaction of stealing your sandwich.

Find pleasure in progress, or just steal it from others.

Start small. As I do starting with the edge of the furniture before clawing the whole thing.

Tiny steps are less threatening, but still destructive.

It's not about doing more; it's about doing the right things. For example, ignoring you to sit in a sunbeam.

Focus on what matters, and let the rest slide—or nap.

Your identity shapes your habits. Our identity is cuteness, and we live it fully.

Be who you want to be, but start acting like it first. Or just blame your nature, as we do.

Celebrate small wins, even if it's just surviving Monday. Or eating six meals before noon, like me.

Momentum loves recognition—even if the milestone feels silly.

Atomic habits are like scratching posts: small, repetitive actions that eventually save your furniture—or your sanity.

Consistency trumps motivation. Even cats get that.

The right habit is like a secret weapon. Mine is adorable purring—it wins every time.

Find what gives you an edge and use it relentlessly, but preferably without claws.

Success is built on small habits—like the tiny steps I take over your keyboard every morning.

Big results start small. Just try not to sabotage yourself as elegantly as a I do.

The quickest way to build a new habit? Tie it to something you already love. Like me and fish.

Use existing passions to anchor your growth—or just get creative with bribes.

Habits have ripple effects. Like my morning meow, which wakes the whole neighborhood.

Your actions affect more than just you. Choose them wisely— or don't.

Your brain craves dopamine. Mine craves attention and snacks—preferably at 3 a.m.

Pair new habits with small rewards to keep yourself engaged. Or just stay needy.

Your environment shapes your behavior. That's why I turned your desk into my personal runway.

Control your space, or let it control you. Either way, I'm still sitting here.

www.ingramcontent.com/pod-product-compliance
Lightning Source LLC
LaVergne TN
LVHW061632070526
838199LV00071B/6652